PATRICK MAHOMES

THE AMAZING STORY OF HOW PATRICK MAHOMES BECAME THE MVP OF THE NFL

By

JACKSON CARTER

CleanCoachingBlog.com

D1416474

The lights on the stage were blinding. As he slowly looked across the audience gathered Patrick Mahomes Jr. took a few seconds to revel in the moment. Coming from an MLB family he always knew he was destined for greatness, but no one could have predicted this level of greatness in this sport.

In Patrick Mahomes we will take you inside the mind and show you the full story of how a skinny baseball star from Texas became the NFL's hottest star.

TABLE OF CONTENTS

LEGAL NOTES

Patrick Mahomes

Destined for Greatness

In August, thousands of video game enthusiasts and football fans will be picking up their copy of Madden '20. Gracing the face of that game's cover will be the 2019 MVP and Offensive Player of the Year, Patrick Mahomes II. Mahomes is the quarterback of the Kansas City Chiefs and received these prestigious accolades after completing only his second season in the NFL, the first of which he spent as the backup to Alex Smith. Although many know about Mahomes and recognize his stellar performance on the football field, not many know about where he came from and the fact that the gridiron wasn't always where his heart and passion lay.

Patrick's parents are Randi Martin and former MLB pitcher Pat Mahomes, who Patrick was named after. The two met, married, and later had Patrick on September 17, 1995, the oldest of three siblings, followed later by his brother, Jackson, and little sister, Mia.

During Patrick's childhood, his father, Pat played for 11 seasons in the majors, making his rounds from ball club to ball club from 1993 to 2003 after a four-year stint in the minors. He was called up to the big leagues and spent time with the Twins, Red Sox, Mets, Rangers, Cubs, and Pirates.

While Pat Sr. bounced around the country following his dream, back home, his family cheered him on. Patrick's mother, Randi, stayed and raised the family in Whitehouse, Texas, and although the couple eventually split when Patrick was only six years old, they stayed close and remained good friends through everything, providing love and support to this day with their close-knit family ties.

Being a professional athlete obviously took Pat away from Patrick's life quite a bit. However, Patrick was able to spend a bit of time with Pat at the various clubhouses that he played at throughout the years, making visits during practices and getting to see what it was like to be a pro.

The influence that Patrick's father and an athletically-inclined environment had on Patrick is one that can be traced back to those childhood moments. Watching his father play on the television and being surrounded by high-performing athletes had a huge impact on Patrick. In fact, Patrick's godfather is another former MLB pitcher, LaTroy Hawkins. Hawkins and Pat played large roles in Patrick's life from an early age, Hawkins even spending a winter with Patrick while his father was in Puerto Rico.

Pat and Hawkins still maintain that bond and support today. Hawkins and Pat attend every single one of Patrick's games together, cheering on the young man and athlete that he has become. When asked about his godfather during a recent interview, Patrick recounted that Hawkins truly symbolized, for him, what it meant to be a professional athlete who showed what it took to play at his peak for a long time. Hawkins was in the league for 21 years, maintaining his health, fitness, and composure in a way that Patrick marveled at from a young age.

And that wasn't all that his father and godfather brought into his life. When he was a child, Patrick was able to rub elbows with other pro baseball players. He hit balls with Alex Rodriguez and even fielded for Derek Jeter. This look into the dedication and hard work required to play at a professional level are things that stuck with Patrick for the rest of his life.

He recounted a time when he saw Rodriguez and Jeter spending hours and hours out on the field and in the cages, perfecting their swings, batting off tees, and working in a way that both confused and amazed Patrick. It blew his mind, at this age, to see someone like Jeter, who was hitting home runs and making stellar plays, spending so much time focusing on hitting off a tee. But this was just the beginning of Patrick's realization that it was exactly that sort of detailed dedication that made Jeter able to perform the way that he did on game day.

Hawkins believes that much of those early years contribute to the way that Patrick is able to succeed and has succeeded throughout his career. Being able to see how professionals act around each other, the camaraderie, teamwork, and dedication were all things that Patrick had the opportunity to witness as he grew up.

He began to see through all of these examples of professional athleticism in his father, godfather, and other greats, that being a professional athlete wasn't something that you accomplished and then rested upon. Instead it became clear that you needed to work harder than ever at that level, Patrick saw, and those who did were the ones who shined when it came to game time. The guys who stayed late and mastered the basics, the ones who didn't rest on the laurels of their current talent, but who knew what it meant to have the pressure to perform on their shoulders and what it takes to deliver on that.

Additionally, it was those athletes that cared about their teams, not just their stats that made impactful performances wherever they went. By watching not only his father and godfather in multiple settings, but the way that those two interacted with their teammates, took care of their health and fitness, and played like true ball players for the good of the team, Patrick began to see what being a professional truly meant.

However, some may argue that these are the kinds of opportunities that most kids just don't get, giving Mahomes an advantage that would naturally lead to his domination in sports. Of course, he's good, some might say, look at his dad, look at the opportunities that he's had to be around the pros, "normal" kids don't get those kinds of opportunities. Additionally, skill plus opportunity can sometimes lead to an inflated ego, issues pop up with being able to handle criticism or defeat, and the ability to stay grounded, especially in the face of the press and criticism that would undoubtedly come with his abilities and background. Thankfully, Patrick's support system and family made sure that he didn't fall to these types of issues, even starting when he was a child.

Knowing this, his mother, Randi, was always concerned about making sure that he stayed grounded, being as humble as possible despite the one of a kind opportunities that his life afforded him. She and Pat had also seen the hard parts of professional athleticism and what it could do to some people when the light was shined upon them in a favorable way as well as in a negative one.

Young Patrick's ego and mindset were always things that Randi worried about as he began to play competitively as a young child. He did well, and she knew that she would need to act now in order to help maintain that humility that she hoped he would carry with him in the future. She claims that she could tell at just seven years old that Patrick was destined for the pros, but she still had hopes for him that he would have more opportunities academically than she or Pat did - Pat was drafted right out of high school, and Randi never went to college. That dream was always on the list of her hopes for Patrick as well as his ability to stay grateful for where he came from. She helped to raise him with modesty in the way that he behaved both on and off of the field.

As he grew, Patrick's work ethic and skill shone. Whether because he had a professional athlete for a father, the exposure to the work habits of top players, or because he just loved the game that much, Patrick was able to compete on the baseball field, and not just at his own level.

Patrick was able to hold his own with those older than him, he not only played with them, but beat out kids two or three years older than himself for the starting position as shortstop when he was only nine years old. Even at this age, his parents could tell that he simply enjoyed playing baseball, plus he had the skill and background to be good at it. His father always hoped that this love and drive to play baseball would carry on throughout Patrick's life, but, like Randi, knew that Patrick would have to choose his own path in life, even if it wasn't lined with baseball diamonds and pine tar.

Finding the Right Fit

Patrick attended his hometown school, Whitehouse High School in Texas. He began truly showing his athleticism's potential in high school, picking up any sport with ease and skill. Those who watched him knew that he could have probably picked any sport to compete in and done well in it. Everything from high jump to ping pong, Patrick's ability to translate his natural talent into success were obvious to everyone.

He played three sports in high schools, balancing the hectic schedules of jumping from one season to the next and still managing to make great appearances in the basketball and baseball seasons as well as playing football. Patrick was a four-year letter winner in baseball and a three-year letter winner in football and basketball, his natural athleticism and drive making him successful in multiple sports.

At this point, though, he thought about quitting football, focusing only on baseball and basketball instead, because football was his least active sport, but his mom talked him out of it. She still wanted him to be involved, balanced, and without the pressures of having to follow in his father's footsteps by only playing baseball.

He was interested and good at playing different sports and having to play and work hard year-round was an opportunity to stay driven, motivated, and busy. Also, since he did so well in basketball and baseball, continuing to play football enabled Patrick to have the chance to sit the bench or take on a more supporting role instead of the show-stopper. It was here that he could possibly learn some of that humility and modesty that she hoped he would gain. Little did she know, how that decision to stick with it would affect the rest of his life in such an amazing way.

Still, this busy schedule, plus school work and his home life responsibilities prevented Patrick from attending the specialized camps where most recruiting is done. By this age, many athletes in high school begin to specialize, spending all of their time and effort in the one sport that they believe they are best at or have the best chances in. This strategy enables them to be able to attend these kinds of special camps, do extra off-season workouts, and play for teams outside of school. All three of these things lead to better exposure.

However, Patrick seemed to be doing just fine. In regard to his basketball career, he took on a strong role and contributed to many successes that his team had. He led the team to a 28-7 record his senior year and averaged 19 points and 8 rebounds - a great presence on and off the court for his teammates. This sport also provided Patrick with the experience in split-second decision making that just didn't get as much of from baseball.

Basketball was also a great chance for him to take a leadership role on the court, making plays and leading his team to victory, but never doing it all by himself.

Both of these skills would end up translating very well into his athletic career later on.

During the playoffs his senior year, he scored 37 and 49 points during in the two games his team competed in. Although the team didn't take the title, Patrick's presence had some believing that his future may end up on the basketball court instead of the baseball field. In fact, most people asked believed he could have gone Division 1 in basketball too, he was simply just a talented athlete who could pick up and perform at a high-level in whatever sport he tried. His godfather, Hawkins, even asserts that basketball was Patrick's best sport, claiming that Patrick could have taken on both Pat and Hawkins at the same time and still come out with the win.

For baseball, Patrick played all three outfield positions, shortstop and pitcher, his multi-sport athleticism also showed up in the various positions on the baseball field as well. He was able to respond with the reflexes and pace of a shortstop, but also the arm and mobility of an outfielder. Additionally, he showed up on the mound and honed a 95 MPH fastball, making him a versatile and effective defensive threat as a part of any team. Playing all four years on varsity for baseball, he was an instrumental part of the team all four years.

Offensively, he showed up almost every time he came up to the plate. He batted .400 as a senior and even managed three home runs that season. One of his friends and teammates from high school and college even commented that he could only recall ever seeing Patrick strikeout a couple of times in the 10 years that they played together.

So, Patrick was a fan favorite and sight to behold no matter what he was doing on the field. This resulted in him being selected as an All-State athlete twice and a four-time All-District player. Pat, his father, had also been an All-State pitcher in high school, so for many, Patrick was proving that he was indeed capable and, on the path, to follow in his father's footsteps.

By Patrick's freshman year, Pat had retired from playing baseball professionally. Instead, he spent a lot of his time making sure that he made it out to all of Patrick's games during his high school career. This ability to have his father around him as he tackled the next level of competition helped Patrick flourish. Not only was Patrick used to seeing his dad work hard, now his dad was around to help Patrick take his own game and work ethic to the next level. This seemed to spell out a successful future in the MLB for him.

In fact, one scout told Patrick his base projected earnings would be around $1.6 million for his career in the MLB. As the son of a former pitcher and a standout athlete himself, his numbers brought scouts to him despite him not being able to go to all of the specialized camps due to the other sports he played. Plus, the ability for Patrick to play multiple roles, one of them including pitcher, only stimulated scouts more because of his potential to be successful and pan out in multiple ways. More teams would possibly take a risk on him because of his upbringing and versatility.

His senior year, Patrick even threw a no-hitter. He threw 16 strikeouts in that game, keeping the opposing team and even a future #33 pick for the MLB from getting a hit in the game. And that was just the first of two games in the doubleheader that day. In the second game of the day he went three for four, batting and almost completed the cycle, a feat that even the pros have a hard time accomplishing. Usually, double headers end up leading to fatigue and a less vigorous effort from players as the difficulties of keeping the adrenaline and physical stamina up become harder and harder. But, even after throwing so well in his first game, Patrick was still a force to be reckoned with in the second.

Later that season, Patrick led the Whitehouse High baseball team to the state semifinals, putting up great numbers in every position that he played. By this time, it was clear that what he had learned from watching his dad and godfather in the pros was about more than just how to play well and perform well, he was able to begin stepping into a leadership role, too. Scouts, fans, parents, and teammates could all see that Patrick had something special in his ability to play as part of a team. It was this quality of leadership and teamwork that many said made Patrick a stand out person, not just a great and talented ball player. The team ended up the year with a 23-8 record that year.

The Tigers drafted Patrick straight out of high school, just like Pat was when he was a senior. There is no doubt that his father was excited about this and hoped that Patrick would follow in his footsteps and continue playing baseball, whether going into the pros or choosing to continue with it in college.

Such a big choice as a senior also brought a lot of concerns in the minds of his parents. Still, they told him to follow his dreams, knowing that they'd done a good job of making sure that Patrick would make the decision that he knew was best for him. His dad even told him, when asked, to follow his dreams, and that everything would end up being figured out on the way. In the end, he decided to forego the majors, and ended up playing a little in college.

THE TRUE PASSION

Despite his success on both the basketball and baseball fronts, Patrick had become more and more interested in football since starting middle school. His former coach believed that it was a chance for Patrick to show some independence at the pivotal teenage age. Baseball was something he'd been living and breathing since his early years. But football was something new, something unknown. And as far as schools go, Patrick was at a school that lent well to someone as athletic as he was.

Whitehouse High had an established football program, with former graduates going to big football colleges like Texas A & M and Oklahoma. During his freshman year, he was the quarterback for the freshman team. The following year, he was the backup quarterback and racked most of his game time playing safety instead. However, in his junior year, he became the starting quarterback for varsity and put up numbers that made a few coaches turn their heads and check him out.

It was at this point, his father said, that Patrick's love of baseball started to take a back seat to his newfound passion for football. It was this chance to be the leader on the football field that really accelerated his career as a quarterback. That year, he was named the Texas Association Press Sports Editors Football Player of the Year. Similarly, it was a chance for Patrick to play something he was passionate about and make a name for himself, not necessarily needing to be referred to as Pat's son like he was on the baseball field.

By the time that he was a senior, Patrick helped lead the team to their first district title in school's history. The team ended the season 12-1. Patrick passed for 4,619 yards and had 50 touchdowns that season. On top of that, Patrick rushed for 948 yards, running in 15 touchdowns of his own. His 95 MPH fastball from the pitcher's mound moved over into a precise, strong arm when he put his pads on.

He was ranked as a 3-star recruit, someone that was doing well at one of the known "football schools," but many look back at that rating today and wonder why he wasn't ranked higher. Similarly, he was labeled as the 12th best dual-threat quarterback in his class, was named AP 4A Offensive Player of the Year, and All-East Texas Most Valuable Player. He was also listed as a Rivals Texas Top 100 Player and a Blue Grey All-American. Despite these accolades, there weren't as many offers for scholarships as many who saw him play would have believed.

However, there was one set of coaches who really had their eye on Patrick. One coach, who was initially interested in Patrick eventually moved on to Texas Tech, working under Kliff Kingsbury, and the two of them soon realized that they had a similar vision for the future of the Texas Tech football program. They both had a great feeling about Patrick Mahomes II.

Kingsbury, who had coached Johnny Manziel previously, knew that Patrick fulfilled his hopes for a mobile, athletic quarterback to add to his team, but also recognized and understood the charisma and leadership that Patrick would bring to the team, even as a freshman. And so, they began pursuing Patrick, even arranging things with the Tech baseball coach to allow Patrick to play both football and baseball, something that is rarely done, or even possible for many athletes.

Patrick weighed his options, considered everything that lay in front of him at that time, and really considered what his future would hold. And when he turned to his parents about the decisions, they both knew that they had to hold their tongues a little bit.

Pat, who hoped that Patrick would play baseball professionally one day, didn't want his own past and career to be the deciding factor for Pat, so he simply told him to do whatever he believed his heart was telling him to do. Similarly, Randi and Pat both hoped that this offer and opportunity for Patrick to get a college education, something that she and Pat had missed out on, would sway Patrick away from the MLB draft and into the path that she hoped for him. In the end, he committed to Tech in April, a whole 10 months before he could actually sign the letter of commitment to the school.

So, even though the Tigers drafted him out of high school, Patrick was fully ready to pursue his football career, while still managing to play a little baseball on the side, at Texas Tech. Only two other schools, both in Texas, offered Patrick a scholarship to play football, leaving many today hard-pressed to see why. His senior year, many of his stats were improved upon from his junior year, but still, only Houston and Rice extended offers to Patrick. However, it was clear, even then, that Patrick had his mind set and seemed to be the perfect fit for what lay ahead of him at Texas Tech under Coach Kingsbury.

Still, it would be very difficult to see anyone look back at Patrick's high school career, both academically and athletically, and think that anything better could have happened. He was a top athlete, no matter what jersey he decided to put on. At the end of his senior year, Patrick was even named the MaxPreps Male Athlete of the Year for accomplishments in all three sports. His work paid off, a rare award and a true testament to his ability, but also his work ethic and love of sports. All of these things and more, set him up nicely for the next chapter in his life, and his accomplishments, dedication, and skill grew even more with the next level of competition.

ESTABLISHING A LEGACY

In the fall of 2014, Patrick was headed to Texas Tech, donning the Red Raider #5 jersey as he watched from the sidelines. However, hopes were high that he would make a home at Tech, filling out and learning enough to one day take over the program and make it into the vision that Kingsbury had for his team. Despite only having two years of starting experience in high school, Kingsbury knew that Patrick was a natural passer, and he also had the multi-sport skills that lent him speed, mobility, and agility that could make him a great addition to the program.

When looking back at the types of quarterbacks that Texas Tech was known for, Patrick didn't seem to check all of the boxes. His 6' 2" frame and 225-pound build paired with his specific set of movement and throwing capacity made him an interesting recruit for the school. However, it was clear that Kingsbury had a vision for Patrick's career there. Kingsbury was a former Texas Tech quarterback and was in his first few years as a coach there when Patrick arrived. Similarly, he continued to hope that with some development, his work ethic, natural athleticism, and ability to lead a team would all come to fruition at Tech in the next few years.

Many young players, especially those hoping to play in college, would have participated in specialized camps meant to develop a player for a specific position. And although Patrick did not attend these camps, he had somehow made it a long way in his short time playing as quarterback anyways. Kingsbury and coaching staff saw the potential in a young, relatively new but incredibly talented, player like Patrick. They could take his natural skill and their experience would develop a winning combination that would fit the needs of Patrick and the team at the same time. One strategy for doing this, was to have Patrick serve as the backup to Davis Webb.

Webb was ranked as a 4-star prospect coming out of high school, while Patrick was only ranked as a 3-star. This would be a perfect opportunity, everyone believed, for Patrick to be able to watch and learn from someone who had been able to make it at this level of play and do it well. Webb had also done a lot to prove his worth as the team's starter, but it hadn't been easy, so there was a lot that he could teach Patrick both on and off the field.

After suffering a bout of the flu that left Webb weighing 40 pounds lighter in just a few days during an earlier season, Webb was already on the path to recover to full-strength but maintained the ability to stick with the team and his role as starting quarterback. However, when that was then paired with a torn ligament and a season-ending ankle injury, Webb didn't have a choice but to sit out and watch as the true freshman came in and took his spot. This gave Patrick the opportunity to show the world, and the Texas Tech fans, what he could do. And he showed them enough to earn himself a permanent spot as the starting quarterback.

Patrick made his debut for the Red Raiders against Texas. He ended up going 13 of 21 for 109 yards that game. He also threw an interception as his team approached the red zone, but he displayed his ability to move around in and out of the pocket, evade tackles, and sling passes down the field. He looked like he'd been playing against these older, veteran players all of his life. Kingsbury saw something in him then, the mobile and level-headed quarterback that he'd been hoping for, and Patrick really began to develop in that position as the season wore on.

Patrick started the rest of the games that season, and although Webb had started the first eight games of the season, Patrick still managed to turn heads with the numbers he was able to put up. Against Baylor, Patrick even threw for 598 yards, breaking the Big 12 record for a freshman passing yards during a single game. In those seven games that he started, he completed 56.8 percent of his passes, racked up 1,547 yards, 16 touchdowns, and four interceptions.

For Patrick, this was the start to his illustrious career at Texas Tech. However, for Webb, it spelled out another story. The numbers Patrick put up as a true freshman, and the potential that Kingsbury and the other tech coaches saw in him were just too good to pass up and Patrick earned himself the starting spot for good. Webb, now finding that his injuries and illness caused him to lose his shot, decided to transfer during the next season and continued his education and football career at Cal before joining the NFL.

Patrick, on the other hand, settled into his spot at Tech and never looked back.

Additionally, that year, Patrick made a few appearances on the pitcher's mound of the Tech baseball team as a relief pitcher. He didn't play more than a few innings in a few games, not even batting, but he was still keeping his options open, allowing him to still express his love of the game, honor his father's legacy, and continue to hone his skills at the next level of play. And he was getting a college education while he was at it.

Sophomore Year

His sophomore year, Patrick was named the starter right out of the gates and went on to play the entire season as the starter. He gained more and more experience and responsibility as the season went on. He started to develop under the coaches' careful ministrations of technique, know-how, and in-game experience. He was even allowed to check into plays by the end of that season, showing that he was more than just a great athletic specimen, he was able to think and strategize on the field as well.

And his skills and stats continued to increase as he played. During the first game of the season, the Texas Tech Red Raiders faced off against the Sam Houston State Bearkats. Patrick threw for 425 yards and completed four TDs during that game. One of those touchdowns was the result of a 64-yard pass from Patrick in the first quarter, giving Texas Tech a lead that they ended up keeping the rest of the game. In the end, the Bearkats fell to the Red Raiders 59-45.

During the second game, he threw for 361 yards and another four touchdowns. He even managed to run in two more touchdowns of his own as they faced off against the University of Texas, El Paso (UTEP). Both of his rushing touchdowns occurred in the second quarter of the game, one for only one yard, the other for 12, both were a result of Patrick leading his team down the field quickly and efficiently and then capitalizing on the momentum that he led them with.

Patrick even sat out at the end of the game as Texas Tech brought home the win against UTEP with a staggering 69-20 win.

For those who were following the college football scene, this was the year that Patrick really began to make a name for himself. He made some stellar plays that season, like an across-the-body throw and even blocking to earn his running back more yards against Arkansas. His ability to put himself on the line for the good of the team resonated well with his teammates, even if it made his coaches nervous.

Even at this point, where he was still an underclassman in a leading role, he knew what he needed to do to fulfill his role, but also what was good for the team as a whole. Clearly, the lessons of leadership and camaraderie that he'd seen and began building in high school were coming to fruition on this bigger stage.

It was clear by the end of this season that Patrick was on his way to becoming a great quarterback. Many watched him as he scrambled across the field, only to find a receiver who could run it into the endzone or tracked Patrick's throws as he made some epic and accurate tosses down the field. He ended up finishing the season with 4653 yards. He also had a hand in creating or scoring 36 touchdowns and 15 interceptions that season. He had taken the success that he had in the end of his freshman year and began to grow as a leader and a playmaker.

On the baseball diamond, Patrick was still not getting very far, though. He didn't make many appearances in games or produce many worthwhile stats when he got the chance to, and in the end, it proved to be the end of the era of his life that revolved around playing baseball. At the end of that baseball season, he decided to quit the team and only focus on football. However, even though he was dropping the sport that had been his passion since a young boy, and the one that had been a huge part of his and his father's lives for so long, he felt like he was following his dream, just like his parents had hoped he would.

JUNIOR YEAR

Going into his Junior year his confidence grew, his teammates respected his abilities and decisions, and the coaches were even more trusting. In fact, that year, the coaches gave him even more responsibilities, allowing him to audible into any play he wanted. In this way, his ability to see things on the fly and make adjustments that would help his offense be successful grew tremendously.

On October 22, 2016, Patrick faced one of the greatest challengers that he would face while wearing the Texas Tech uniform when they faced off against Baker Mayfield and the Oklahoma Sooners. In an offensive battle that proved to be an incredible display of quarterback versatility and talent, Patrick and Mayfield went back and forth down the field throwing over 500 yards a piece. When watching the highlights of that game, it is clear to see that Patrick and Mayfield each had their own set of skills, but that both showed their arm strength and accuracy in amazing ways. They both also displayed an affinity for reading the field and making adjustments as the game went on. In just the first half, the two quarterbacks had put a total of seven touchdowns on either side of the scoreboard.

In the end, the Red Raiders fell to the Sooners 66-59. Mayfield finished the game with seven touchdowns and 545 passing yards. Patrick, however, threw five touchdowns and an outstanding 734 passing yards. This tied the record for passing yards thrown in a single game. However, Patrick also racked in another 85 yards rushing, bringing his total yards in that game up to 819, setting a new record. Because Mayfield was pretty much a shoo-in for the NFL, so this was one of the first big tests of whether or not Patrick's natural talent could show up when faced against a quarterback of such a high caliber.

Although the scoreboard said otherwise, anyone who watched the game or took a look at the stats knew that Patrick did more than just show up, he competed and showcased what he was truly capable of. For many, who know how much of a power Oklahoma is in the football world, the fact that Patrick and the Red Raiders stayed so competitive spoke a lot to how Patrick led his teammates in that game. Also, just the fact that Patrick racked up over 800 yards in a single game is a testament to his hard-working style and is an amazing feat, especially in a college matchup.

Together, Oklahoma and Texas Tech broke the Division I all-time, single-game yardage record with 1,708 yards from both teams. Also, Patrick managed to break a record that hit a little closer to home. By completing 52 passes in a single game, he beat out the former record holder, Kliff Kingsbury when he was a quarterback at Texas Tech, who was now standing on the sidelines and calling the plays for Patrick. No matter who you were cheering for that night, it was definitely one to remember. Fans, coaches, and even scouts had their eyes on the game that night as two top-tier quarterbacks faced off and began to raise questions about what their futures might hold if they wanted to eventually go pro.

By the end of his junior season, Patrick showed the country that he was the real deal, improving from the years previous in big ways. In fact, he even led the country in a number of stats. He averaged 421 yards per game, had a total of 5,052 passing yards for the season, and a total of 5,312 offensive yards. He was also responsible for 318 points and a total of 53 touchdowns. He was honored with the Sammy Bough Trophy for best college passer and was named as an Academic All-American, 2nd team player.

After accomplishing all of these things and managing to break a few records along the way, he sat down with coaches and parents and discussed his future. In the end, he decided that it would be in his best interest to move on to the NFL and declared for the draft instead of finishing his senior year. He was still able to graduate, however, at the end of only his third year with a 3.91 GPA. His mother, who had hoped the most that he'd be able to get a college degree, was able to watch her son excel on the football field but also in the classroom.

For a young, talented athlete like Patrick, it could be very easy for him to slack off in the classroom, resting at the bare minimum needed to be eligible to play. However, that wasn't good enough for him. He hit the books as hard as he hit the field, and both Randi and Pat watched their son complete his college career with proud smiles on their faces.

At the end of his career at Texas Tech, Patrick was revered by many as one of the great quarterbacks to come out of Kingsbury's system. He joined the rank of others who ended up in the NFL after being coached by Kingsbury such as Case Keenum, Davis Webb, Johnny Manziel, and Nic Shimonek. Many saw him as a potential first or second round pick in the NFL, and when he decided to move to the NFL, a lot of people considered him one of the greats, if not the greatest quarterback to ever come out of Texas Tech.

However, whenever there are standouts like Patrick that come out of college early and head into the draft, there are always concerns about whether or not they will pan out. Only time would tell if Patrick had what it took to take his level of play to the ultimate level and face off against seasoned defensive linemen and go toe to toe with Superbowl winning quarterbacks.

At the Texas Tech pro day, 28 NFL teams showed up and watched as Patrick displayed his skills. This is a pretty impressive number given the fact that they were mainly there to see Patrick only, and many of the other schools that had turnouts of that number were places that had multiple prospects that scouts would be interested in.

Over the course of the workout he threw about 80 passes and completed 74 of them as he threw a multitude of long and short passes. He commented that he attempted to showcase a variety of skills, like being able to work under a variety of circumstances. His agent said that Patrick did a great job of showing the pro scouts that he was capable of adapting to a new style of game.

To top it off, Patrick belted out an 80-yard pass at the end of pro day to show off his big arm. He said that it was all his idea to pull off this Hail Mary style throw at the end of the day. It was his plan to display all of his skills, even the ones that aren't typically tested at a pro day event. After taking a few steps to get his momentum going, he tossed the ball 80 yards to the opposite endzone and into the hands of the awaiting receiver. In an era of Aaron Rodger style passes to win a game, Patrick believed that it couldn't hurt to show the scouts that he was fully capable of pulling off something similar if given the opportunity for one of their teams.

However, Patrick's true goal that day was to show the NFL teams that he had more to offer than just great passing skills. He wanted them to see his passion for the game and his dedication. He hoped that they took in his leadership skills as well as his arm, his ability to work well with a team as well as his overall stats. It was a great showing for him, and many teams were rumored to have been interested in signing Patrick, making him feel like he had done everything that he could to show teams what he was all about.

A Dream Come True: The NFL Draft

The Air Raid System is an offensive system in which the quarterback works out of a shotgun and can audible based on what he sees at the line of scrimmage. This type of system is more popular in college football, and, it would seem, Kingsbury had built Patrick for that sort of system. But looking at others who had come to the NFL out of Air Raid offenses, it is easy to see why there would be those who doubted whether Patrick's skills in that type of offense would translate to the more complex beast that is professional football.

Along with that, some believed that anyone out of the Air Raid System, which tends to favor passing plays, may lack the ability to comprehend complex defensive formations in the pros or even be able to make the passes they need to under the intense situations that an Air Raid built quarterback might find himself in when facing a top-notch defensive line.

Coming out of the combine, nobody doubted his arm or his strength and mobility. In fact, he threw 60 MPH passes, tying for the fastest ever recorded. However, there were some who saw his style and noted that he'd developed habits that were less than enticing for an NFL scouting for his team. His decision-making skills and ability to play under a coach who may not allow Patrick to take the reins as much as he may have become used to at Tech, were all concerns that

NFL teams considered as they saw how Patrick performed before the draft.

Compared to others in his class, he was ranked by Sports Illustrated as the 2nd Best QB prospect. According to ESPN, he was 3rd Best, and NFLDraftScout.com put him at 4th Best in his class. And yet, many reported that they felt like Patrick was years away from being ready to play. He was projected as a first or second round, and many more vocal people believed that the second round would be most likely.

Following the Texas Tech pro day in which he threw the 80-yard pass in front of 28 teams, he was invited by 18 of them to have private workouts and visits. This, along with a review of his stats and the performance he gave at the combine, made Patrick one of the fastest rising prospects during the pre-draft process. There was definitely a buzz around his name, but he had plenty of those who doubted he's payoff as well.

On the day of the draft, Patrick and his close family and friends gathered in a country club in Texas. He had chosen not to attend the actual draft in Philadelphia and believed that he may have to wait until the next day (in the third round) to even hear his name called out by a team. However, his agent, Leigh Steinberg, didn't doubt for a minute that he'd be picked a lot sooner than that. In fact, he was selected at number 10 overall.

The Kansas City Chiefs had already expressed their interest in picking up Patrick, but they didn't have a pick until 27. Team executives had already begun to talk to other teams with higher picks, but there was nothing in place that could land them Patrick, who they believed would definitely be selected prior to their pick. And as the hours ticked by and the first nine teams selected their rookies, Chief chairmen, Clark Hunt bit his nails. And so, when the first nine picks came and went, and Patrick was still sitting with his family and friends unclaimed, they went ahead with a trade they had in place with the Buffalo Bills.

The Chiefs gave the Bills their 27th pick, the third-round pick, and their first round pick the following year. This move required the approval of the owner due to the fact that they were giving away a future first-round pick. But Hunt approved. And they got Patrick.

Thankfully for the Chiefs, they managed to outmaneuver other teams that were rumored to be interested in Patrick such as the Saints, Cardinals, and Giants. The Saints had the number 11 pick, so the Chiefs just managed to squeeze in ahead of them and snag Patrick, who they believed to be the best quarterback available. The Chiefs surprised almost everyone with their trade move and subsequent pick. Even the Bills representatives said they had no idea who they were trading up for and couldn't believe that they were even looking at a quarterback while Alex Smith was on their roster.

In fact, Patrick was the first opening round QB draft pick by the Chiefs since 1983, when they picked Todd Blackledge. The team typically favored veteran quarterbacks and liked to spend their picks elsewhere. In addition, they currently had a veteran quarterback in Alex Smith, but some in the organization wanted to begin planning for the long run and felt that Patrick could learn from Smith and then transform the team. However, the team and staff knew that Patrick offered something different and that they needed to pick him up.

Coach Andy Reid commented that the draft room had been pretty tense leading up to their pick, and that they all knew that Patrick could make a huge difference for their team. He also shared that the team knew that there were others that were going to actively seek Patrick in the draft, but when the Chiefs selected him, it was a special moment in their draft room. Reid stated that there wasn't a single person in the room who didn't see the value of Patrick and not a single one who believed that selecting him was the wrong choice for the team.

The buzz that had begun around Patrick had proven to be true. He went as the second of only three quarterbacks to go in the first round, following the Bears second overall pick of Mitchell Trubisky and preceding newly selected Texan Deshaun Watson at number 12.

When interviewed after being selected, Patrick was just happy to be finally living his dream. He revealed that when he first started playing in high school, it had always been in his mind to try and get the opportunity to play football professionally and get drafted. This was a day that he had been looking forward to for a long time, and he was glad that he'd been able to experience it while surrounded by his family in friends.

INTO THE FOLD: ROOKIE YEAR

Patrick signed a 4-year, 16.42-million-dollar contract with a signing bonus of 10.08 million. He joined the reigning AFC West Champions and spent his first year as backup to Alex Smith, who was beginning to hit a great stride in his career. The coaching staff and ownership were all excited to work with developing Patrick and allowing him the ability to watch and learn from Smith. Patrick felt secure in the fact that he knew what it means to work and wanted to impress the Chiefs and Coach Reid with his work ethic. And, it seems, his hard work paid off.

When the Chiefs secured their playoff spot with the number four seed, they decided to rest Smith and Patrick got his first start in Week 17 versus the Broncos. This was an unprecedented move as the Chiefs hadn't started a rookie at quarterback since 1979 except for during strike games. Patrick knew, before the game, that he needed to go out there and prove his worth, show the team and the world that he was capable of playing at this professional level.

And he could. After working with Andy Reid and Mike Kafka personally, Patrick came into the game against the Broncos and showed them what he was made of. He was set up with a bunch of other backup players as the starting lineup was resting for the playoffs and had their sights set on the coming weeks. However, Patrick came out and fired off a 35-yard pass through a tiny gap and directly into the hands of his covered receiver. It was the kind of throw that showed not only his timing, readability, and power, but it showed the accuracy he had as well. Many veteran QBs would be hard pressed to complete passes in that narrow of a margin and in such intense coverage. It was clear from the get-go that Reid had a lot of confidence in Patrick as he set him up right from the start with three passing plays.

Later in the game, the blitz came to put pressure on Patrick, and he managed to scramble and evade being brought down until he threw across his body and about 30 yards down the field. It seemed then that the power of his arm paired with the focus and versatility that he brought to the field were a winning combination. In the end, he went 22 for 35 and 284 yards. Reid and the rest of the staff were excited and satisfied by his performance and looked forward to what it could mean for the future. Patrick led the Chiefs to a 27-24 victory and made an impression that would last and pay off into the following season.

INTO THE BIG TIME

Most NFL Analysts thought Patrick's second season would be something like his Rookie season. But, the Chiefs continued to surprise the NFL world when they traded Alex Smith to the Redskins and named Patrick as their starting quarterback. It was only his second year in the league, and he had only started one game. But everyone on the Chiefs sideline was excited to see the direction that Patrick's arm and leadership would take the team. It seems that he was able to ingratiate himself into the dynamics of the veteran players, make a strong, lasting impression to teammates and coaches, and interested the owners into making this decision.

In the game against the Los Angeles Chargers, Patrick didn't disappoint. In a showcase of his ability to move the ball down the field and deliver on one big play after another, Patrick showed everyone that he wasn't just a fluke. He was the real deal. With his momentum and drive, his ability to scramble out of the pocket and still make progress, he led the team along with Tyreek Hill as the Chargers fell to the Chiefs 38-28.

For many who watched him play, it signaled the start of something magical for the Chiefs. As an offense, it seemed the players trusted that Patrick was willing to do what it took to continue plays even if plays began to unravel. He added a new level of threat to the offense, where defenses had to be sure to defend against the running power of players like Kelce and

Hunt, but still be aware that Patrick could run or even turn a short run into a play down the field. He threw for a total of 256 yards and 4 TD passes, finishing the game with a passer rating of 127.5. This great display of his skills earned him the AFC Offensive Player of the Week recognition.

The very next week, the Chiefs faced off against the Pittsburgh Steelers, and again, Patrick delivered. He threw for 326 yards that game, completing six touchdowns and had a passer rating of 154.8. He actually tied the Chiefs franchise record of most touchdowns completed in a single game, tying Len Dawson with six. The buzz that had followed him through the pre-draft process was beginning to really grow again. All over the sports media outlets, people were talking about Patrick's performances and the way that he was stunning football fans everywhere. He ended up winning the AFC Offensive Player of the Week again that week, becoming the first quarterback to win the recognition two weeks in a row since Tom Brady.

And the greatness didn't stop there. In fact, Patrick managed to break the record for most TDs in the first three career games and even won AFC Offensive Player of the Month in September. In a Monday Night showdown versus the Rams in Week 11, Patrick threw for 478 yards and another six touchdowns. He led his team to a 12-4 season and continued to show everyone that the Chiefs were a force to be reckoned with. By the end of the season, Patrick had thrown for the most yards of any quarterback during the 2018 season, beating out passers like Rodgers and Brady.

He even became one of seven players in the history of the NFL to throw for 5000 yards in a single season. He became the first Chiefs player to throw for over 300 yards in eight consecutive games. He also led the league in passing touchdowns. With his performance, he led the Chiefs to a division title, amazing everyone by his ability to perform at such a high-level after such a short career. And his family was there to support him every step of the way.

Patrick's godfather, Hawkins, attended all of the games with Patrick's father, Pat. Pat, who was a MLB pitcher, a position notoriously known to be superstitious, actually wore the same outfit to the first five games of the season because Patrick was doing so well and the team was winning.

It wasn't until they came up against the Patriots in Week 6 that they suffered a loss. So, Pat was able to change outfits again, but Hawkins commented that if the Chiefs had continued to win, Pat would be fully comfortable with wearing the same shorts and shirt to the games well into the colder seasons, if it meant his son was out there doing well. Pat even mentioned that he was so nervous for Patrick when he first began playing, but as soon as he saw his son take the field and make some of those great plays under pressure, his doubts left him, and he realized that although Patrick had chosen pads over a glove, Patrick had made the right choice. The football field was exactly where he should be, and he was proud of him. Patrick was even spotted sporting his father's old Mets jersey when he showed up for one of his games, proving that the superstition may be on Patrick's mind as well, but the support and love of his family is.

When it came to the playoffs, Patrick and the Chiefs continued their trek to get as far as they could. Nobody questioned Patrick the same way that they had at the beginning of the season after Patrick had shown off his skills and drive. In the Divisional Round, the Chiefs faced Andrew Luck and the Colts. It was a brutal battle, and many were excited to see how the Chiefs would fare. But in the end, it was a pretty uneven match as the Chiefs took the win with a 31-13 score. Many then predicted that the Chiefs were going to take it all the way that season, some even guaranteeing that there was no way that Patrick and the Chiefs would be beaten by the Patriots in the next round.

However, it wasn't that easy. Veteran coach Bill Belichick and soon-to-be-dubbed greatest of all time, Tom Brady were not going to just let Patrick get to the Superbowl without trying to make it a fight. The beginning of the season, many analysts discussed the need to reevaluate and adjust defenses for any team hoping to meet the Chiefs in the playoffs, otherwise they'd be in for a hard matchup. It seems that Brady and Belichick, along with the rest of the Patriots' were prepared for what they were coming up against. In a battle back and forth that eventually led to overtime,

Patrick went toe-to-toe with Brady, going 23 for 36 to Brady's 24 for 35. He racked in 352 yards to Brady's 340. He threw two interceptions, but seemed, to many, to be performing at a level well beyond his years of experience. He even completed four touchdown passes to Brady's one, but in the end it wasn't enough. The Patriots took over in overtime and scored a field goal to take the win, ending the Chiefs season and chance for a shot at the championship. Still, many dubbed the match up the true Superbowl showdown, seeing this as the game that they were excited about the most in the playoffs.

After the Chiefs season was over, though, the buzz around Patrick didn't die down completely. Patrick was named a Pro Bowl selection that year and later managed to snag the title of 2018 NFL MVP, adding to the shine and glory that he'd brought himself and his team that season. Many were now praising Reid and Hunt's decision to trade up for Patrick, many even talking about the fact that, if it could be done again, there would be no way that Patrick should have been anything but the number one overall pick in the draft based on how he panned out in the pros. And nobody seemed to have any regrets about letting such a young, unproven quarterback take full reins after coming off of a few successful seasons with a veteran quarterback.

And that wasn't the only news that Patrick made that year. A meme made its rounds through social media about Patrick choosing to put ketchup on everything, and someone close to him even mentioned that he began to refrain once he had so many eyes watching every move he made because he didn't want it to be something weird or odd about him in the news. However, it turned out to be a boon for him as Hunt's Ketchup picked up on it and offered him an endorsement after realizing his love for their product.

Later, Patrick was even named the Cover Athlete for Madden NFL 20, earning him an honor that is incredibly rare, especially as such a young player. He also made appearances supporting the Texas Tech basketball team during March Madness and continued to make headlines by supporting and inspiring the team to give it their all in the tournament as he watched with other fans in the stands.

Overall, it was a standout year for Patrick, both on and off of the field, and many are looking forward to where he will go next. However, he still manages to stay humble and realistic in interviews, making sure that everyone understands that the success of himself and his team are not resting on his shoulders alone. In fact, he constantly makes it a point to highlight the team he is a part of, both the one that he wears the jersey for, and the one that has built up around him throughout the years.

Surrounded by his family, his high school sweetheart, and the many, many fans that he has now made, it is clear that Patrick's future is bright. Even now, the buzz is building about him and how he will perform in his next season after such an eventful first season at the helm of his team. Chiefs fans and just football fans alike will be anxiously awaiting to see what Patrick has up his sleeve and whether or not he can maintain the momentum that he built at the beginning of his career for as long as he cares to put on the uniform and get out on the field.

AUTHORS NOTE:

Let us remember the real purpose of writing someone's biography. The job of the author is to help the reader know better the person about whom we are writing. To read all the facts that should be told and their imprint on this life right now. The whole of their life needs to be told, even the smallest points that include the way they felt, their thoughts, their ideas, determinations, good and bad deeds. Unfortunately, not everything that could make an impression upon the reader can be included in a book, but the fundamental elements that form that character are there to make a difference maybe even in your life. The author must make sure it is all told, the good, sad, bad and the unfortunate as it builds the character of the person and what turned them into who they were/are in life and how those experiences caused their life to contribute to the world in which we live. Everyone has a purpose during their time on this earth, and each leaves their imprint on others' lives in some way, sometimes that imprint may not be noticed until far into the future. Remember, we have but one chance of traveling through this life and make a difference.

MORE FROM JACKSON CARTER BIOGRAPHIES

My goal is to spark the love of reading in young adults around the world. Too often children grow up thinking they hate reading because they are forced to read material they don't care about. To counter this we offer accessible, easy to read biographies about sportspeople that will give young adults the chance to fall in love with reading.

Go to the Website Below to Join Our Community

https://mailchi.mp/7cced1339ff6/jcbcommunity

Or Find Us on Facebook at

www.facebook.com/JacksonCarterBiographies

As a Member of Our Community You Will Receive:

First Notice of Newly Published Titles

Exclusive Discounts and Offers

Influence on the Next Book Topics

Don't miss out, join today and help spread the love of reading around the world!

OTHER WORKS BY JACKSON CARTER BIOGRAPHIES

Made in the USA
Middletown, DE
06 April 2020